JANUARY, 2002

THE TEMPLE OF KONARAK

Konarak, Temple of the Sun, Orissa. Thirteenth
century A.D. Maithuna.

THE TEMPLE OF KONARAK
EROTIC SPIRITUALITY

Photographs
ELIOT ELISOFON

Text
ALAN WATTS

London
THAMES AND HUDSON

To Joseph Campbell

Designed by Norman Snyder

First published in Great Britain in 1971
by Thames and Hudson Ltd, London

Printed in the United States of America

ISBN O 500 23140 0

INTRODUCTION
Konarak

I had just finished photographing several long views of the Sun Temple of Konarak and was setting up my camera for a close-up of sexual union between two figures beautifully carved in stone when my assistant, a young, well-educated Hindu from New Delhi, placed himself between the sculpture and my camera. He pleaded with me not to take the photograph. When I asked why, he answered, "What will Americans think of us when they see this picture?" He was not alone in that opinion. Many Indians were and some still are ashamed of the erotic subject material which adorns this temple. There are other temples which include erotic sculptures, but only two, Konarak and Khajuraho, are noteworthy. I have photographed both, Konarak four times and Khajuraho once.

I first visited Konarak in 1949 when the incident described took place. I was engaged in photographing the major Hindu and Buddhist architecture and sculpture of India which I illustrated for Heinrich Zimmer's *The Art of Indian Asia*. This extensive coverage gave me the opportunity to judge Konarak in a vast panorama, to realize fully its beauty, both for its architecture and its sculpture.

Konarak. Detail from south wall corner.

The temple is south of Calcutta in the modern state of Bhuvaneswar, called Orissa during the medieval period. It was built by Narasimha Deva of the Ganga dynasty in the thirteenth century A.D. on the shore of the Bay of Bengal, but the sea has receded several miles since then. It is in the classical north Indian style which consists of two principal structures, a high tower called a *sikhara* and a smaller building, the *mandapa*. In Orissa the *sikhara* is known as the *deul*, and the *mandapa* as *jagamohan*. There are often other smaller buildings forming a temple complex surrounded by a stone wall.

The *deul* of the temple at Konarak fell down centuries ago. There is a theory that it collapsed while still under construction because of its enormous weight resting on soft ground. The overall structure of the *jagamohan* is fairly well preserved. It is a square building in the classical Indian style, a hundred feet long on each side and a hundred feet high. The building has been designed to resemble a huge chariot belonging to Surya, the Sun God, and there are twelve-foot-high stone wheels, six each on the north and south sides of the temple. Seven life-size horses were sculptured in the round in front of the structure, several of which remain. There are also two attendant elephants.

This building has a lower portion, about half its height, called the *bada*. The *bada* originally had a statue of the Sun God Surya in a niche on each side, but only two are still in position. Unlike the soft sandstone the temple was built from and which has been partially eaten away by the elements, the human-size statues of Surya were carved in hard dark-green chlorite, and are among the finest Hindu sculptures extant.

The upper half of the *jagamohan* is called the *pida* and consists of a series of three tiers diminishing in size to form a pyramid which is topped by a round cap called the *amla*. There is a shallow platform circling the structure above each of the three tiers. The lower two form a stage for a group of female musicians carved slightly larger than life size in the round. The top one has several mythological lions still in position.

The temple of Konarak displays a range of mediocre to inspired sculpture. The hardstone statues of the Sun God and the life-size figures of lovers set high on the sides are beautifully carved, but some of the erotic friezes on the lower terraces are extremely clumsy. The overall elaborate filigree pattern is as delicate as lace. One of the finest effects is the continuous frieze of elephants around the base.

Hindu temples usually have an innermost shrine in which the *lingam*, a stone phallus about two to four feet high, stands upright in the center. It is a simple circular column rounded at the top. The *lingam* symbolizes Siva, one of the paramount trinity of Hindu gods. It is sometimes placed on a circular stone with a hollow center called the *yoni* which is the female counterpart of the *lingam*. Many of the *lingam* are very smooth and shiny at the top from the constant ministration of milk and oil by devotees. The *lingam* at Parasure Amesuara temple near Konarak is adorned every morning with a red hibiscus blossom.

I had timed my visit to Bhuvaneswar to be in Puri, the closest rail point to Konarak, during the Rathayatra festival at the temple of Jaganath. This temple is the largest one of the medieval period and is considered one of the most holy in India. Each year during the month of June, the wooden bust of Jaganath, another name for Krishna, and busts of his sister Subhadra and his brother Balbhadra, are taken out of the temple to another one on the outskirts of Puri. There have been as many as one hundred thousand pilgrims here during this festival. Thousands drag the huge wooden chariot from one temple to the other, holding on to two long ropes attached to its frame. Police guard the chariot to prevent fanatics from throwing themselves under the wheels to reach eternal bliss.

In southern India, west of Madras, the great teacher Sri Ramana Maharshi reclined every day on a stone bench in full view of the hundreds of devotees who came to be in his presence. He rarely spoke, but honored me when he mentioned to his disciples to observe my working with the camera. I had been extremely quiet, moved slowly and tried to take my photographs as unobtrusively as possible. He mentioned that, as well as drawing attention to my hands and how they held and worked the equipment. This encouraged me to make an unusual request. Since he was old and very infirm at that time, it was impossible for him to walk without a cane and some assistance. I had learned of his first pilgrimage to Tiruvanamalai and the sacred mountain of Arunachala near where the Ashram is built. I asked if I could photograph the master with the sacred mountain as a background and he made this effort for me on the last day of my visit. To be in a master's presence is called *Darshan*, and I was as moved as the throng who sat before him.

My second visit to Konarak was in 1956. I was en route to the South Seas after a European assignment for *Life* magazine, and Calcutta was a convenient layover. From there one can either take the overnight train to Puri or fly to Bhuvaneswar on Indian Airlines in ninety minutes. I wanted aerial photographs of Konarak, and also had so little time that I chartered a single-engine plane piloted by a Captain K. L. Krishnan, the flying club instructor at Bhuvaneswar, to take me to the temple, which had a primitive airstrip near it. I made use of the flight to photograph some of the countryside on the way to Konarak to establish its orientation. I was also able to do an aerial of the largest temple in this region, and one of the holiest shrines in India, Lingaraja, which means king of the *lingam*. As at Puri, non-Hindus are not permitted inside the surrounding wall of the temple but may mount a wooden platform built outside which is slightly higher than the wall in order to see the buildings and temple courtyard.

My third visit to Konarak was providential. I arrived at the temple on a Friday afternoon, April 21, 1961. I made some photographs of the façades, which were best by afternoon light, and retired early. I was awakened at dawn by the sound of many excited voices near my window. I looked out and saw hundreds of people on the temple grounds. A dozen visitors a day in those days would have been unusual. This swarm was extraordinary.

I soon learned that by a remarkable stroke of fate I was at Konarak on *Sanipooja*, the day that Saturn and the moon were in the correct relationship to contact the planet. Pilgrims were at the temple accompanied by priests to give thanks to Saturn, which they consider malevolent, for sparing their lives. Small groups sat around fires tended by the priests pouring ghee into the flames as an offering.

The keeper of the bungalow pleaded with me not to rush outside with my cameras. He explained that these were simple country people who might take offense at my presence, let alone my photographing them. I began by working from the window with various telephoto lenses, but I soon realized that this would never do and that I had to go outside. I began slowly, never approaching too closely to any group. I had read enough newspaper stories about people being killed in India by religious fanatics—although I was no Moslem. I managed to do some work when I made the mistake of taking more than one quick photograph of a lovely woman carrying a beautiful child across her hip. I was observed by her husband who started angrily toward me. I began to take pictures of him as he approached and, when he was fairly close, beckoned him to sit down on a rock so I could do his portrait. He was so pleased that he forgot about my photographing his wife.

I also made photographs of the temple itself, many with the pilgrims. From the first terrace, there were opportunities to relate these human figures to the statuary, giving a sense of scale.

I was again in India in 1962 photographing the Taj Mahal at Agra. Khajuraho is less than half a day away by car, and I decided to go there for the weekend. The visit produced a portfolio of photographs which is included in this volume. As I have noted previously, both Konarak and Khajuraho share the same architectural style and erotic sculpture embellishing the exteriors.

Khajuraho is a complex of more than a dozen separate small temples, within walking distance of one another. They all have the typical *sikhara* and one or more *mandapas*. The most interesting one of these is Kandarya Mahadeva which was built about A.D. 1000. The *sikhara* is 115 feet high, and there are three connected *mandapas* of successive heights leading up to the tower. Except for the upper half of the *sikhara*, which is carved in vertical ribs, the buildings are covered with horizontal bands of statuary. These are figures of divinities and humans in the round, but still attached to the stone panels from which they were carved. Unlike those at Konarak, these sculptures are in almost perfect preservation and are a feast to the eye. Most are subtle and delicate—a tender embrace, a loving look, a soft caress. But there are three panels in which the act of copulation can only be described as acrobatic. These groups are high up on the façade but were easily photographed with the telephoto lenses I had brought with me.

I made what I hope will not be my final visit to Konarak in November of 1968. It was still possible, even during this fourth visit, to see and photograph the architecture and sculpture of Konarak with interest and enthusiasm. The enormous stone chariot of Surya, the Sun God, is truly a masterpiece in the history of art. It is a perfect illustration of that profound Hindu thought, *Boga is Yoga, delight is religion.*

ELIOT ELISOFON

Konarak. Another view of erotic couples on base of *shikhara.*

(*Next page*)
Konarak. Air view from north. To the left, ruins of *nata mandir*, the dance hall. Center, *mandapa* over entrance chapel. Right, ruin of fallen main tower (*shikhara*). The complex of *mandapa* and *shikhara* represents chariot of the Sun God. Wheels along the sides and steeds in front.

Konarak. *Mandapa* east front (restored).

Konarak. Attendant elephant.

Konarak. Musician figures from south wall of
nata mandir.

Konarak. *Nata mandir.* View from roof of *mandapa.*

21

Konarak. Standing figures from roof of *mandapa*.

Konarak. Chariot wheels, south side of ruined
shikhara. Predominantly erotic figures shown here,
in contrast to the dancing and drumming figures
shown on page 21. Shrine of the Sun God, center
at top level.

Konarak. First horse on the south side in front of
chariot.

Konarak. Nagas—the serpent couple, or serpent king and queen.

Konarak. Surya. The Sun God.

Orissa. Holy man with lingam.

Orissa. Procession on behalf of Vishnu, Jaganath, "lord of the moving world." A modern day folk celebration with a car of the deity, suggestive of the great nearby temple of Konarak, which was an expression in the eleventh to thirteenth centuries of an aristocratic cult.

People of Orissa at a festival.

(*Next Page*)
Tiruvanamalai, Arunachaleshvara mountain.
Temple from the west. Twelfth century A.D.

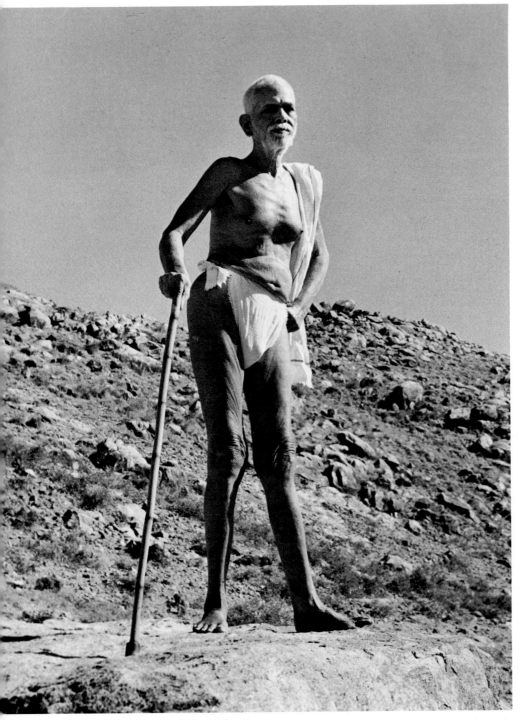

At foot of sacred mountain Arunachaleshvara.

Sri Ramana Maharshi at his Ashram.

Rice paddy with looming Lingaraja temple on
horizon.

Sirshasana (Head-stand Posture)

Akarna Dhanurasana (Shooting Bow Posture)

Mayurasana (Peacock Posture)

Dhanurasana (Bow Posture)

Festival of Saturn, when the planet is closest to the
moon, with the Temple of Konarak in background.

A temple in the Orissa style. *Shikhara*: large tower at left, next to *mandapa*.

Bhuvanesvar. Mukteshvara temple circa A.D.
950. Shiva temple to the lord of spiritual release.

Ornamental detail. Serenity amidst the squirming
flesh and gnawing teeth.

(*Left*)
Details from Orissan temples.

(*Right*)
Apsara, or heavenly courtesan.

(*Next page*)
Bhuvaneshvara. View of the great temple compound. Eighth to
thirteenth centuries A.D. Lingaraja temple towering in center.

52   Bhuvanesvar. Celestial nymphs (Apsaras).

Figures from Rajrani temple, circa A.D. 1100.

Bhuvanesvar. Figures including monkeys and pet
bird from Rajrani temple.

EROTIC SPIRITUALITY
The Vision of Konarak

For many years there has been a growing fascination in the West with Indian spirituality—a subject which is, nevertheless, still widely misunderstood, both here and in India. For most Hindus have little more comprehension of Hinduism than Christians of Christianity, and we should no more be surprised at the platitudes of swamis than at those of parsons. Generally speaking, the exponents of Hinduism that a Westerner is likely to meet will be Brahmins (that is, members of the clerical caste) with an English-style education roughly following the curricula of Eton and Oxford. From such exponents he will almost invariably learn that there are two essential prerequisites for any deep understanding of Hindu wisdom: you must abstain from sexual intercourse and from taking any form of animate life. These are the basic virtues of *brahmacharya* and *ahimsa*, requiring that you become a celibate and a vegetarian.

Thus, to Indians with this background the erotic imagery of their ancient temples is as embarrassing as the *Bhagavad-Gita*, and both are explained away with considerable humbug. The *Gita*, the discourse on the battlefield between Krishna and the warrior Arjuna, is regarded quite rightly as an epitome of the most profound Hindu doctrines. Yet one of its main points is that there is no necessary inconsistency between being a warrior and a yogi, between using the sword and following the way of spiritual liberation. Today it is, of course, explained that the battlefield of the *Gita* is in fact the human mind, and that the enemies whom Arjuna is to slay are simply our own passions and evil propensities. But if that be the case, why does not the *Gita* say so? There is nothing so esoteric about this admonition that it needs to be veiled in symbolism.

Similarly, one will be told that erotic sculpture has nothing to do with sex, except insofar as sex itself, like battle, may be employed as a symbolism of higher things. Thus the male and the female represent spirit (*purusha*) and nature (*prakriti*), the Godhead and the cosmic illusion (*maya*), or the pairs of opposites (*dvandva*)—such as light and darkness, life and death, being and non-being—and that their intercourse likewise represents spiritual realization of the basic unity of the cosmos. Yet if this be so, why the luscious and exuberant sensuality which still glows through the battered statuary of Konarak? Imagine, then, these images in their original state, with the stone polished and painted in vivid color. If the message is simply and solely that man and woman in intercourse are types and shadows of cosmic unity, why the frills, the multiplicity of postures, the cooperation of attendants, and the detailed variations of genital play?

Modern apologists for these images are doubtless right on one point: that they are pornography only in the eyes of people with dirty minds. We are not looking at some ancient version of a "stag film" or "girlie" magazine, for their faces are innocent of the leer which always masks shame and guilt at finding "pleasure in filth." There is no attitude, here, of secretiveness or of intent to shock by doing openly what should be done in the dark. Yet if their function is simply to portray innocent eroticism, or to be a form of sex-education for a public without books, why do they cover a whole temple, and why does their iconographic imagery make it plain that they are *both* symbolic *and* erotic in equal measure?

These, then, are the problems of this essay accompanying Eliot Elisofon's marvelous photographs of Konarak and its sculptures. I am not going into the archeological and iconographic details of the temple (a project on which a great deal of fieldwork remains to be done) nor into a minute and scholarly discussion of the erotic lore of India.[1] My purpose is to describe a context or perspective in which these simultaneously erotic and spiritual manifestations of ancient Indian culture may be understood, not merely as museum pieces and survivals of obsolete attitudes to life, but rather as expressions of a philosophy of enormous importance—and, indeed, interest—to the modern world.

This means that we must go beyond and behind the subtle disagreements of Hindu and Buddhist scholastics, in all their varieties, and try to get a glimpse of what Sir John Woodroffe called the *bharata dharma*—that is, the *Weltanschauung* or world-view of ancient India, of which the many forms of Hinduism and Buddhism are different aspects (*darshana*). For the importance of studying cultures other than our own is to get down to their basic assumptions and feelings about the world and thereby—based on a sort of triangulation between their views and ours—bring reality itself into clearer sight. This is, of course, a form of the academically despised art of generalization, whereby those who see forests rather than trees, or wholes rather than parts, are barred from scholarly discourse.

We must first explore the fundamentals of the Hindu view of the

1. For such matters the reader is referred to the following: Heinrich Zimmer, *The Arts of Indian Asia* (2 vols., Pantheon Books, Bollingen Series, New York, 1955); Alain Danielou, *l'Erotisme Divinise* (Editions Buchet/Chastel, Paris, 1962); Philip Rawson, *Erotic Art of the East* (G. P. Putnam's Sons, New York, 1968); Agehananda Bharati, *The Tantric Tradition* (Rider & Co., London, 1965). This last is the most thorough and well-informed discussion of Indian traditions of erotic spirituality as yet published, but we should not neglect the much older work—Sir John Woodroffe, *Shakti and Shakta* (Ganesh & Co., Madras, and Luzac & Co., London, 1929).

world as expressed in such sacred writings as the Upanishads, some of which date from at least 800 B.C. Our difficulty here is one of terminology, because the first Sanskrit-English, and Sanskrit-German dictionaries were compiled under the assumption that, as of the latter part of the nineteenth century, there existed in the West philosophical and theological terms which could faithfully translate their supposed equivalents in Sanskrit. Such dictionaries misled not only Westerners but also Indians who, lacking missionary zeal for converting the British to Hinduism, had compiled no Sanskrit-English dictionaries of their own, but rather accepted ours on trust. They therefore swallowed the idea that Hinduism is a "religion" in the same sense as Christianity, that the highest reality is "spiritual" as distinct from "material," that the *atman* is the "soul" or "self," that *brahman* somehow corresponds to the concept of "Godhead" (with its monarchic and imperial overtones), that *citta* is "mind" or "consciousness" as differentiated from "body," that *sunyata* is ultimate "nothingness" as understood in Western nihilism, or that *maya* is a word equating what we mean by "illusion" with what we also mean by "the material world."

It was thus that we fabricated a notion of Hindu philosophy as a mixture of Berkeley's Idealism, solipsism, and Christian Science—and many Western-educated Indians fell for it. What it came to was that the world we see and feel is a falsely imagined dream. So long as we take it for reality we are in suffering and terror, as one who, in the dark, steps on a rope and mistakes it for a serpent. Those, however, who are awakened from this dream know that reality is one boundless, formless, and timeless light, apart from which nothing else exists. But this awakening can come about only through rigorous control of the mind and emotions, so that all attachment to the material world is eradicated. Whoever achieves this awakening realizes that he is identical (i.e., one entity) with God, and thus attains the divine attributes of omnipotence, omniscience, and omnipresence.

The difficulty is that this caricature of Vedanta, the central doctrine of Hinduism, is not wholly false. It must be corrected by getting rid of all Western ideas signified by the words "spiritual," "material," "soul," "body," "real," "unreal," "God," "world," "mental," "physical," and so forth. From the start it must be understood that Hinduism, as exemplified in Vedanta or Yoga, is neither philosophy nor theology, nor even psychology. It has nothing to do with establishing certain beliefs or conceptions to be held as Truth. The focus is on immediate experience, not ideas. Considered as a method, Yoga is therefore a way of correcting our perception of reality, of learning not to confuse what we perceive with what we conceive.

To clarify this point we must make a preliminary distinction between reality and symbol, which corresponds somewhat to the difference between wealth and money, territory and map, events and their description in words. We all know how to see, even if we cannot describe the physiology of vision. In the same way, we all know "reality;" but because it is not something verbal we cannot put it into words. Thus to think that reality is "material" is to confuse it with a philosophical idea, and the same is true in thinking of it as "spiritual." Ideas and concepts are, indeed, real; we form them as we form tools and numbers. But the reality *about* which we form ideas is not itself an idea: it is more like a sensation or a feeling — that is, an experience.

Thus, to get at reality the Western philosopher refines and complicates his concepts. The Hindu abandons his concepts so as to "become again as a child" and experience "what there is" nakedly and directly, without, however, any philosophical notion that "experience" is something which confronts or is encountered by an "experiencer." Such differences are constructed by thinking, by separating experience into bits (i.e., things and events) designated by words, and then imagining that experience really is such an amalgamation of bits. Hence, what we call the world of material things and events the Hindus call *nama-rupa* literally "name-forms," between which the separations are nominal— as between the two ends of a pole—rather than actual. If we confuse the world of separate name-forms with the real world, we imagine that reality is itself disjointed and disintegrated; but if we see that name-forms divide reality into bits only as the clock divides motion into separate minutes, then our view of experience is integrated and whole. Thus the world, or reality, as seen undivided by name-forms is the *brahman*, the absolute, which cannot be defined as spiritual or material, eternal or temporal, one or many, this or that—whereas when we have reality confused with the separate name-forms we are trapped in *maya*, the world-illusion.

This is difficult to understand only as we try to grasp it intellectually. It must be approached through Yoga. And to try to understand Vedanta without doing Yoga, in one or more of its many forms, is as absurd as trying to experience the Himalayas simply by reading travel books. The *Yogasutra* defines Yoga as *citta vritti nirodha*, which means, approximately, "being aware without thinking," for Yoga is initially the temporary suspension of the habit of talking to oneself, of the compulsive cluttering of naked experience with words and ideas about it. Yoga is not blank-mindedness or unconsciousness: it is simply silence of the mind, and we break that silence as soon as we attempt to say *what* it is that we realize in Yoga. If you listen to music openly and attentively, with closed eyes, you cannot *hear* any difference between the music and the listener. If you look at a view you cannot *see* any difference between the view and the viewer. It is only a concept, an inference, that sounds and sights "impress" themselves on your consciousness as if it were a slate or a mirror. Such concepts simply vanish if you are simple, honest, and truthful about what the experience actually is—if you do not confuse the experience with what you have been told and brought up to think about it.

None of this is meant to imply that words, thoughts, and ideas are evil and should be shut out of mind. The point is that they are good as servants but bad as masters, and to be in control of them we must from time to time send them away. Of course, the idea of an "I" which "sends" them away is itself a thought, and it, too, vanishes in the state of Yoga. Since such concepts as past and future also vanish, the present is no longer called the present. It follows, also, that in Yoga one is not seeking any result, any change of consciousness, any special experience, since these are all notions apart from what actually is now.

We, who live in a civilization where mental silence is almost nonexistent, regard thinking and busy-mindedness as our principal claim to humanity. We believe that a mind without thoughts would surely be a regression to infancy or a descent to pure animality. But, ironically, our consistent confusion of symbols with reality ends up with plastic people, routed from the maternity ward to the crematorium like battery-farmed chickens. For unrelieved thinking turns everything, oneself included, into mere objects. If you begin with the principle that what cannot be classified and symbolized does not exist, you arrive at a destination where only symbols are real, and today we have just about arrived. One does not have to be a philosopher to know when bread is no longer bread and beer is no longer beer, yet most Americans are unaware of the difference. When the swift and systematic destruction of the planet is called progress, we have taken leave of our senses.

Contrary to general assumptions, Yoga is a highly sensuous undertaking. It is a *sadhana*, which is to say a discipline or practice (somewhat like swimming or dancing) having little to do with philosophy or theology as understood in the West. But, if Yoga is sensuous, if its concerns are concrete rather than abstract, how can it be called a "spiritual" discipline and how can we speak of *samadhi* (the untranslatable term for—horrors!—"yogic consciousness") as an experience "beyond the senses?" The problem is strictly semantic. Yoga is a purification of the senses from their bondage to concepts, for which reason the highest form of *samadhi* is called *nirvikalpa*, that is, *nir-* (non-) *vikalpa* (conceptual.) Thus, among the concepts from which sense-experience is to be purified are precisely our ideas of things, bodies, entities, objects, beings, and even sense-organs, none of which are contents of direct experience. If this is an affront to common sense, it goes only to show how thoroughly and deeply we are in bondage to symbols. Yet, when I am described as "looking at an apple" or even as "looking at energy appling," my actual experience has already been falsified by leaving out the background or field in which the apple is seen. Looking at an apple is a conceptual, intellectually selective operation; what I actually see is infinitely more, and no amount of words could ever describe it. If we restrict knowledge to what can be said, thought, or conceived, we box ourselves into a pitifully abstract, finite, and lifeless world. And yet we say that we *know* how to see, how to walk, how to breathe, or how to listen without being able to explain it at all.

The reason, then, why so many Westerners and modern Indians are entirely frustrated in their attempts to practice Yoga is that they are in search of some "spiritual" experience (by which they really mean "abstract") beyond or apart from what is immediately sensed, and sometimes manage to hypnotize themselves into a catatonic trance where they are altogether senseless, imagining this to be *nirvikalpa samadhi*. It can hardly be said too often that Yoga is liberation from *maya*

(illusion) when the illusion concerned is the confusion of reality with concepts, the impression that one is actually experiencing a multiplicity of separate things, entities, bodies, events, and so forth. Actually *maya* is based on the Sanskrit root *matr-*, to measure, signifying "the world as measured or metered" and thus the world considered as bits or things. Obviously, meters, inches, hours, and ounces have no concrete reality except as calibrations on instruments, but it is less obvious that bodies, things, and events are devices of a similar order.

On what ground, then, can it be said that the practitioner of Yoga realizes "union with God" or "identity with *brahman?*" Certainly this has little to do with "God" in the monotheistic sense of ruler, king, or personal boss of the universe. It is simply that when disentangled from concepts one's awareness (no longer "mine") is—so to say—integrated, undivided, or "non-dual" (*advaita*). It is beyond measure, beyond the antithesis of knower and known, beyond every kind of categorization. When this state is thoroughly realized, talking and thinking will no longer interfere with it, and the yogi will have no difficulty in working and communicating with others in the normal way—except that he is no longer under the spell of symbols.

The actual discipline of Yoga consists of various *upaya* or "devices" to bring about the temporary cessation of conceptualization. The two main difficulties are, first, that symbolic thinking has become a compulsive habit and, second, that the very intention of stopping it is itself a thought. Therefore, practicing Yoga with the intention of gaining liberation is rather like trying to surprise oneself. However, this latter difficulty is more verbal than real, and there is nothing for it but to plunge in. One must bear in mind that Yoga is not "practice" in the sense of preparation, as when one practices the piano for a concert. It is rather "practice" in the sense of practicing medicine, that is, of following a vocation or way of life which is its own goal.

The principal *upaya* or device of Yoga is usually translated as concentration, but this word must not be understood in the sense of *straining* attention so as to hold it fixed upon a single object. Yoga is relaxed concentration, used simply as a technique for absorbing awareness with something other than thoughts. This may be done through vision, by looking at a point of light; through hearing, by listening to a meaningless sound; through proprioceptive touch, by feeling and regulating the breath; or even through smell, by the use of incense. One does not think about the object of concentration: one simply feels it until there is nothing in mind but the feeling. It helps to sit with the back erect to avoid sleep, and to have the eyes, the tongue, and the forehead relaxed since all symbolic thinking is accompanied by subtle tensions in these areas. In due course one can be in this kind of concentration without any specific object at all.

Concentration-without-object (*asamprajñata*) can also be approached by a still more relaxed method. If we compare awareness with a pool of water and conceptual thinking with ripples or mud, it will be obvious that ripples cannot be smoothed out with an iron, nor mud settled by pushing it to the bottom with the hand. If the pool is left alone it will become calm and clear by itself. The equivalent is to let the ears hear whatever they hear without naming the sounds, to let the eyes see whatever they see, to let the lungs breathe as they will, and to let thoughts flow along aimlessly if they must—treating them, however, just as noises and figures in the head of no more meaning than the sounds and patterns of flowing water.

The specific method or type of Yoga is varied to suit individual temperament. Thus *karma-yoga* is an absorption in physical action without regard for its "fruits" or advantages, and is similar to the Japanese use of judo, fencing, archery, brush-painting, or tea-ceremony for the

It is worth noting that psychoanalysis is an application of psycho-hydraulics, being based largely on the analogy between psychic functions and the behavior of water, where the Id is considered as a vast libidinous tide or river, dammed by the ego under the direction of the superego. If the dam provides inadequate outlet for the stream, the contents of the Id are repressed and the dam is in danger of a break, as in the phrase "psychotic break." Or the stream may find itself another course and issue as cruelty instead of sexual love. While there is nothing inherently objectionable in the analogy, it must be remembered that Freud's hydrology was based on Newtonian mechanics and his conception of the psyche strictly mechanical. Psychoanalysts speak of "unconscious mental mechanisms." It is thus that, under the scrutiny of psychoanalysis, as of behaviorism and conditioned-reflex psychology, the individual becomes an object to himself—an automaton. Newtonian mechanics sees the world as a conglomeration of distinct entities, ultimately billiard-ball atoms, reacting to each other through the mechanism of "causality," as the ball moves "because" struck by the cue . . . and so *ad infinitum*. However, there is no place for the idea of causality when it is understood that the separation of entities from one another is purely conceptual, like the notion of the three dimensions of space or the constellations of stars. Thus understood, the world is at first figuratively and later literally "blown to bits." The causal relationships between things and events are clumsy apprehensions of the fact that they are not truly separate from each other.

Ancient Indian ideals of sexual love differ considerably from ours. As described in the *Kamasutra*, intercourse is a complex and elegant ritual, an act of mutual worship between god and goddess. But the stress is not on male orgasm; it is on male erection, on the prolonged contemplation of erotic tension in union with the female partner. Isn't it immediately obvious that, with this emphasis, erotic pleasure is prolonged and enhanced for both man and woman? If one enjoys the excitement of caressing and entering a woman, why be in a hurry to get it over? But this, like every superior form of pleasure, requires discipline—in this case, a discipline of delight.

One of the most striking features of the Konarak images is that these couples are not "going to bed" or "sleeping" with each other. They are standing or sitting—unless we are to imagine the temple walls as floors. Furthermore, they are not starkly naked, but ornamented with crowns, necklaces, bracelets, and bangles, and, in many scenes, they are not alone. All of which suggests that what they are doing is not felt to be a lewd and dirty pleasure for which one should seek bathroom-like privacy. Their lovemaking is a sort of ritual dance. Our difficulty in understanding this is the feeling that the combination of worship and sex is like water and fire: so religion is blasphemed and lust is quenched by solemnity. But the gestures and expressions of these figures are not solemn, pious, or sanctimonious. Unfortunately we associate religious feeling with the serious loquacity of our own religious observances, for which we don our most uncomfortable clothes, sit penned in pews, and pray frowning with closed eyes.

By contrast, almost all Hindu ritual, whether associated with sex or not, is joyous. The *mantra*-chanting, the gestures and dances, the offerings of flowers and incense—all these seem to express the belief that the universe is the *lila* or "playing" of the Divine, in which we are encouraged to join. Hindu musicians laugh in delight at each other as they increase the speed and intricacy of their performance, whereas the Western concert hall is, like Church, "for serious." Although "holy joy" is declared to be one of the essential virtues of the Christian saint, our expressions of religious joy are almost always pompous, as in the

Konarak. Eroded wall figure in northwest corner.
Apsara.

hymns "Onward Christian Soldiers" and "Jesus Christ is Risen Today."
Indeed, to Indian ears most Western music sounds like a military march,
reflecting a military conception of the universe with a chain of command
going up to:

> God the all-terrible King who ordainest
> Great winds thy clarion and lightning thy sword.

A virtue missing in our religions is the ability to "come off it."

We are, however, looking at a monument of the thirteenth century
produced by a culture which long antedates the Mogul Empire of the
Muslims and the British Raj, for, as I said at the beginning, the modern
educated Indian is, at least in theory, a puritan. Until relatively recently
the very existence of such monuments as Konarak and Khajuraho was
frequently denied; access to them was made difficult and their symbolism was explained away. It is understandable that Hindus would take
offense at Western tourists who came only to snigger and to snap
"feelthy pictures" for the folks at home. But they themselves were, and
are, uncomfortable in the presence of their monuments. C. G. Jung
tells the following story of his visit to Konarak in 1938:

> When we left the temple and were walking down a lingam [stone
> phallus] lane, he [the guide] suddenly said, "Do you see these stones? Do
> you know what they mean? I will tell you a great secret." I was aston-
> ished, for I thought that the phallic nature of these monuments was
> known to every child. But he whispered into my ear with the greatest
> seriousness, "These stones are man's private parts." I had expected him
> to tell me that they signified the great god Shiva. I looked at him dumb-
> founded, but he only nodded self-importantly; as if to say, "Yes, that
> is how it is. No doubt you in your European ignorance would never
> have thought so!"[4]

The guide, incidentally, was a learned Brahmin pandit.

It cannot be denied that there was a strong puritan bias among the
Brahmins long before the reign of the Empress Victoria, but its suppo-

---

4. C. G. Jung, *Memories, Dreams, and Reflections* (Pantheon Books, New York, 1961), p. 278.

sitions differed somewhat from those of Western puritanism. Sex was not dirty or wicked; it was simply inconsistent with spiritual development. It was felt that seminal emission involved a depletion of *ojas* or psychic energy, and Indians tend in general to think of the loss of semen as we think of the loss of blood. There is, in fact, no comparison, but many Hindus take quite literally the symbolism of Yoga as a process whereby the semen-energy is drawn up the spinal column into the brain and thus entirely sublimated. But in India, as elsewhere, the chief achievement of sexual repression is a vast amount of hypocrisy. Having studied such matters for many years, I am of the opinion that the only people who really do without sex are either too old, too ill, or too sated. There are, perhaps, some exceptions, but I can think of nothing more detrimental to spirituality and sanity than forced abstinence from sexual activity.

One major qualification should be added. The genitalia are not the only centers of erotic experience; there are circumstances under which the whole organism can become an "erogenous zone" to such an extent that almost all experience becomes erotic. This is particularly true for an accomplished master of Yoga, for whom sex is no longer "on the brain" as a conceptualized "goodie" which has to be attained at all costs. He can take it or leave it, for he lives in a constant ecstasy in the light of which genital sex simply ceases to be a compulsion. But Europeans and Americans have sex, just as they have everything else, "on the brain." They regard sex as a special "part" of life, as they also regard religion, work, play, or education. But, as we have seen, life has such "parts" only in the conceptual sense; and to the extent that we insist upon their reality it becomes difficult or impossible to cross-fertilize sex with religion or work with play. Religion without sex is a rattling skeleton, and sex without religion is a mass of mush.

But to the old Brahminical superstition that loss of semen was loss of psychic energy there has, indeed, been added a heavy element of British prudery, as is acknowledged, even gratefully, by some Indian intellectuals. Author and critic Nirad Chaudhuri's contempt for his own cultural tradition explains well enough the embarrassment over Konarak:

> The most important of the new concepts with their passional cor-relatives which we acquired [from the British and their literature] were these: first, the idea of God—that is, a personal God of the Christian type. Secondly, the idea of Man, as a being whose personality was a thing of value in itself. Third, the idea of Country, which is of course patriotism as understood in the West. Fourth, the idea of Nature, as an ennobling and purifying influence on the human personality. The fifth is the idea of Love as a relationship between man and woman which was not the creation of the sexual urge: and the sixth the idea of physical Beauty—that is, the bodily beauty of man or woman as a thing of aes-thetic and moral enjoyment, not of sensual feeling. . . . The love which found expression in the mutual self-surrender of both man and woman, which became a spiritual passion based on the carnal, was not known to the Hindus. There is a good deal of rubbish talked about the Hindu love manuals and about the sophistication of the Hindus about the man-woman relationship. Actually the manuals said nothing about love: they are forbidding practical treatises on methods for sexual congress, books which were likely to scare all idealistic persons off love, or for that matter even sexual relations; they are wholly unhuman. The com-ing and adoption of romantic love into Hindu life can be traced step by step from the middle of the seventeenth century. . . . In pre-British days a woman's body was a thing to be leered at and, if possible, slobbered on. The only passion it roused was lust.[5]

Going back beyond the seventeenth century to the fourteenth, we have, for example, the Bengali poet Chandidas speaking of his intensely platonic and courtly romance with Rami, the exquisite but low-caste washerwoman:

5. *The Listener*, vol. 78, no. 2017 (November 1967. British Broadcasting Corporation), pp. 664–5.

I have taken refuge at your feet, my beloved.
When I do not see you, my mind has no rest.
You are to me as a parent to a helpless child.
You are the goddess herself, the garland about my neck,
   my very universe.
All is darkness without you; you are the meaning of
   my prayers.
I cannot forget your grace and your charm, and yet there
   is no lust in my heart.

And then look at the photograph on page 107. If this is not tender, cherishing love, and if the sculptor had no appreciation of the aesthetic beauty of the human form, one's eyes are not to be believed.

How can one *argue*, verbally, as to whether or not spirituality is compatible with sexuality? The question can be answered only by going beyond words, that is by finding out what happens in the sexual relationship when it is performed as Yoga, without conceptualization or seeking a result, such as orgasm. If the word "lust" is to designate a vice, it must refer to a mental attitude rather than an organic process, and it seems to me that lust in this sense is precisely a fetishistic fascination with certain "parts" of the body—the penis, the vagina, the breasts, the buttocks, the feet, the lips, or the nape of the neck. Lust is, as it were, preferring the breasts to the whole woman. Or it is isolating and conceptualizing out the thing "woman" from the setting and context of her whole environment. In the nonverbal state these fragmented fetishes have no reality: the environment, the woman, and every feature of her body are ripples in an unbroken stream, whereas the chopped-up woman—the hair, the bosom, the waist, the bottom, the leg—is Marshall McLuhan's "Mechanical Bride." This mechanical fragmentation destroys woman just as it destroys nature.

Along with its erotic sculpture India has repressed its own tradition of Tantric Yoga in which liberation was realized through the very "things" which are supposed to be its impediments. These are the "Five M's"—*mada* or wine, *matsya* or fish, *mamsa* or meat, *mudra* or aphrodisiacs, and *maithuna* or sexual intercourse. On the principle that "to the pure all things are pure," nothing can be an obstacle to Yoga unless regarded as a "thing." Sex is an obstacle so long as it is obsession with "cunt" or "a piece of ass." Thus destructive lust is inflamed by compulsive veiling of certain so-called *parts* of the body, since this merely draws attention and hypnotic fascination to the parts so kept apart. To a natural person, the statue of a naked man without a penis or of a woman without labia is simply a maimed image with an organ conspicuous by its absence. Tantric Yoga is also called *sahaja*, the art of living naturally and spontaneously without being "blocked" or "hung-up" by various conceptual entities which are supposed to be especially attractive or repulsive—such as love and death. Coomaraswamy defined it as "a perpetual uncalculated life in the present"—considered, however, as the conscious background of superficially necessary calculations, as is the practice of music to the theory of music.

But if we consider practice more *real* than theory, in the same sense that the nonconceptual and nonverbal world is more real than its symbolic counterpart, and that, in Yoga, experience is more fundamental than intellectual understanding, then the "Five M's" can be understood as sacraments rather than seductions. There is all the difference between, on the one hand, taking life as it is given, and, on the other, exploiting it for games in which the ego is calculated to win. Drinking, eating, and sexual intercourse are seductions and impediments to liberation only when used to assuage the hollow agony of identifying oneself with an ego or separate person, as the glutton tries to fill his empty and imaginary soul rather than his stomach.

Otherwise, the "Five M's" are simply the basic elements of life as it is found on this here-and-now level of the play and vibration of energy. *Mada* is wine "which maketh glad the heart of man," "the great medicine for humanity, helping it to forget deep sorrows, and the cause of joy," corresponding to the element of fire. *Matsya* is the food of the sea "which is pleasing and of good taste, and increases the generative power of man," corresponding to the element of water. *Mamsa* is flesh and fowl "which are nourishing and increase intelligence, energy, and strength," corresponding to the element of air. *Mudra* is grain, "easily obtainable, grown in the earth, and the root of the life of the three worlds," corresponding to the element of earth. *Maithuna* is sexual union, "which is the cause of intense pleasure, the origin of all breathing creatures, and the root of the world which is without either beginning or end," corresponding to the element of *akasha* or space.[6] Isn't Christianity aiming at something of the same kind in sacramentalizing bread (*mudra*) and wine (*mada*) in the Eucharist, water (*matsya*) in baptism, and copulation (*maithuna*) in holy matrimony?

The *tantras*, both Hindu and Buddhist, comprise a body of esoteric writings which expound the full and practical implications of the formal doctrines of Hinduism and Buddhism. The word *tantra* is said to be derived from *tan*, "to spread out," and, thus, to develop, to explore implications, to expand, or to bring to full fruition. It must be understood that the basic teachings of the Vedas, the Upanishads, and of the Buddha are not regarded, as are the Christian gospels, as full and final revelation of truth in such a way that any later development is a corruption—to be avoided by going back, as Protestants say, to "the simple teachings of Jesus." The basic "truth" of Vedanta and Buddhism alike is not comprised in doctrine, dogma, or formal proposition of any kind; it is experience, a transformation of consciousness. The doctrines are simply the opening statements of a dialogue between teacher (*guru*) and student (*shishya*), which the latter initiates by raising questions as to the "prob-

6. Cf. *Mahanirvana Tantra*, 7. 103–110. Arthur Avalon (Sir John Woodroffe), *The Great Liberation*, (Ganesh & Co., Madras, 1963), pp. 205–206.

lem of life" as it strikes him. The function of the *guru* is to solve the problem by demonstrating it to be an illusion, a meaningless question, or the exploration of a blind alley. Thus the Buddha "taught" that all suffering (*duhkha*) is the consequence of craving (*trishna*) in order to encourage his disciples to see what would happen, psychologically and practically, if they tried to eradicate craving and found themselves craving not to crave. In the same way, when the late Sri Ramana Maharishi was asked such questions as "How am I to achieve liberation?" he would reply, "Find out *who* is asking the question"; in other words, "Why do you want to be liberated?" For the desire to be liberated, to be "saved" or "enlightened," rests upon the illusion of the separate self which feels trapped in an alien world of "others" and of external things and processes.

The *tantras* are therefore concerned with the practical and psychological experiments involved in working out these questions, and are esoteric in the sense that they cannot be understood without exploring the psycho-physical disciplines which they prescribe. All esoteric knowledge boils down to the experiential realization that the problems of life are simply nonsensical games which you yourself have proposed, similar in principle to trying to have your cake and eat it. Thus Hindus and Buddhists are agreed that such problems, and the torments involved, are your own *karma*—which is to say, problems of your own making or doing, invented out of thin air. To put it in another way, there isn't really a problematic thing called "life," on the one hand, and, on the other, a "you"-entity confronting it. The Hindu formula is *Tat tvam asi*—"You are It." In Buddhist language, "All is *sunyata*," which, though literally meaning "All is emptiness," indicates that reality is beyond every fixed formulation, and that all formulations (such as the distinction between "self" and "other") are empty.

If, then, sexual desire is a form of craving which leads to all the sufferings of infatuation, jealousy, debilitation, and, finally, disillusion when the beloved grows old and ugly, you may try to solve the problem by attempting to get rid of lustful emotions. But you will be trying to flatten the waves with an iron, for every puritanical approach to this problem merely aggravates it to the point where the Demon of Lust wears all the titillating masks of celibates' black habits, or of bustles, crinolines, impenetrable corsets, black stockings and gloves, layers of lacy petticoats, leather skirts, bowler or derby hats, riding boots and britches and whips, and all the bizarre apparatus, with its male equivalent, of Victorian eroticism. By comparison the statuary of Konarak is the play of innocent children.

Tantric Yoga (specifically in the form of *maithuna-yoga*) solves the alleged problem by heading straight into it, saying, "Let us experience the sexual feeling as it is in itself behind and beyond all our ideas about it." In essence, what this Yoga involves is that male and female allow their mutual reactions to be aroused during the preliminary ritual of adorning each other with necklaces and garlands, and offering each other incense and wine. They are, of course, facing each other in the posture of meditation (*padmasana*) with legs crossed and feet soles upward upon the thighs. When the man is fully aroused, the woman embraces him by sitting on his lap and folding her legs around his waist. With her arms about his neck and his hands supporting her back, they look straight into each other's eyes, as in the familiar *yab-yum* images of Tibetan Buddhism. Whatever the precise posture, the point is that from then on there is nothing in consciousness but the wordless sensations of bodily contact, genital contact, eye contact, and the mutual rhythm of breathing. They remain embraced without motion, and allow the intensity of the sensations themselves—or the sensation itself—to suspend all ver-

bal and conceptual thinking, so that there are no longer any notions of "desire" or "sexual intercourse," or of trying to make anything happen other than "what is."

The *tantras* go extensively into the cosmic symbolism of this Yoga, explaining how the couple transcend their John Brown and Mary Smith personalities and realize that behind the façade of their conventional and historical identities they are in fact the primordial pair—Krishna and Radha, Shiva and Parvarti, or, in Buddhist imagery, Vairocana (the central and eternal Sun Buddha) with his consort Akashadhatu Ishvari (the Sovereign Lady of the Dimension of Space). In Hindu imagery the female is the *shakti* or active principle and the male the passive, he the *purusha* (witnessing Self) and she *prakriti* (the natural world), he the *paramatman* (the Self of the universe) and she *maya* (the cosmic illusion which is also creative power). In Buddhist imagery the male is active and the female passive, he is *karuna* (active compassion) and she is *prajña* (clear wisdom), he *rupa* (form) and she *sunya* (the void), he the *vajra* (lightning-diamond) and she the *padma* (lotus).

One can only translate this symbolism into terms that are meaningful in our culture by saying that, in an embrace of this kind, all considerations of time and place, of what and who, drop away, and that the pair discover themselves as the primordial "love that makes the world go round." There is an extraordinary melting sensation in which "each is both," and, seeing their eyes reflected in each other's they realize that there is one Self looking out through both—and through all eyes everywhen and everywhere. The conceptual boundary between male and female, self and other, dissolves, and—as every spoke leads to the hub—this particular embrace on this particular day discloses itself as going on forever, behind the scenes.

At the genital center of the embrace, phallus and vulva form the nucleus of a double helix, which is the pattern of our galaxy. The two organs seem to change and change about in their roles so that phallus becomes vulva, and vulva becomes phallus. Indeed, there exist Tibetan and Nepalese bronze images of this kind which, when separated, disclose the male with vulva and the female with phallus. For there comes a strong physical experience of androgyny, of each sex completing and balancing itself by an infusion of the other. His urge and her surrender, his thrust and her opening, become a single feeling experienced equally by both.

These, of course, are poetic images fashioned after the event. For, as the *Brihadaranyaka* says, "When a man is in the embrace of his beloved spouse, he knows nothing as within and nothing as without," nothing, indeed, of any other dichotomy. When calculation and classification stop there is nothing to be said but everything to express.

If we read the ritual directions for marital intercourse as described in the *Mahanirvana Tantra*, they will seem to peculiarly dirty Western minds as merely funny, absurd, and superstitious unless we can understand the basic intent of Yoga as herein combining both sexual contact (*maithuna*) and sonic vibration (*mantra*) to get into the heart of nonverbal reality. The following is a paraphrase of Sir John Woodroffe's rather technical translation of the text:

> He should then with his wife get on the bed, and there sit with his face towards the East or the North. Then, looking at his wife, let him embrace her with his left arm, and, placing his right hand over her head, let him intone the *mantras* appropriate to the different parts of her body: over her head the *mantra* "*Klim*" a hundred times; over her chin "*A-im*" a hundred times; over her throat "*Shrim*" twenty times, and the same a hundred times over each of her two breasts. He should then intone "*Hrim*" ten times over her heart, and twenty-five times over her navel. Next, let him place his hand on her vagina and intone "*Klim A-im*" a hundred-and-eight times (equals the number of beads on a rosary), and

then the same over his own member. And then, intoning "*Hrim*" let him open her vagina, and let him go into her to beget a child. The husband should, at the time of the spending of his seed, be aware of this event as *brahman*, reality itself, discharging it deeply into her womb, and at the same time intone:

Yathagnina sagarbha bhur, daur, yatha Vajra-dharina,
Vayuna dig garbha-vati, tatha garbha-vati bhava.
"As the earth is pregnant of fire and heaven of Indra,
As space is pregnant of air, so do thou also become pregnant."[7]

For the subjective point of view I quote the following description by a modern Buddhist tantric, C. M. Chen of Kalimpong:

1. During the first stage, when all those love-actions such as the "sixty-four arts" are going on, the personal ego of the man is absorbed into the object of attraction, the beautiful or charming *dakini* [Buddhist term for the *shakti* or female partner]. The man could say, "I would like to die on your body." Nothing of the whole world remains in his mind. Nothing is able to disturb the man's concentration of loving action. Not any kind of *dhyana* [meditation] of the formed or formless heavens could so naturally and spontaneously enable him to forget everything and be rid of every delusion like this concentration of *vajra* [diamond-like] love. It is so pure and unpremeditated and unreflecting. This stage is therefore identified as the *sunyata* [no-thingness] of love, for by loving actions the *sunyata* of personality is experienced and realized.

2. When both productive organs are in contact, the outward vulva encircles the penis, and the inward gnostic small and secret nerve of the vagina is inserted into the urethra. [This seems to be referring to a sensation in the "subtle body" as distinct from the physical, preliminary to what we would call "vaginal" rather than simply "clitoral" orgasm.] Such a double embrace of the productive organs enables the wisdom-energy of the male and of the female to pass through each other, and the wisdom drops, both gross and subtle, are also exchanged, and through these interpenetrative actions the great pleasure of both sexes is increased. They know neither object nor subject in the copulatory action. He forgets subjectivity and indulges only in the oneness of no-personal-ego and no-*dharma*-ego. Thus the great pleasure [*mahasukha*] is identifying with the vast *sunyata* [no-thingness] of love.

3. When the organs come to their climax, both white and red drops

7. Cf. Arthur Avalon (Sir John Woodroffe), *The Great Liberation* (Ganesh & Co., Madras, 1963), pp. 270–271. This *tantra* is from about the seventh century.

of wisdom [*prajña*] and compassion [*karuna*] have been harmonized. Even the [idea of] pleasure is forgotten and the *samadhi* of no-thingness and pleasure mixed alone remains. Simultaneously, the ego-existence embedded in the eighth level of consciousness and accumulated from past lives is forgotten, and there comes the experience of the absence of egocentric pleasure, and with this absence identification with the great *sunyata* is realized.

4. After the emission of the wisdom drops, a man who is very skillful keeps himself without leak [i.e., *ashrava*, and in this case without seminal emission. The "drops" are presumably the mucoid discharges of the organs.] If he keeps the *samadhi* of identification [with no-thingness] the *dharmakaya* light [or the "clear light" of *sunyata*] will appear. With the full identification of *sunyata* and *mahasukha* [supreme bliss], full enlightenment is reached. There is no longer any "highest realization" [*samyak sambodhi*] to be pursued.[8]

In the second quotation the writer is discussing, not marital intercourse with the aim of reproduction, but *karezza* or *coitus reservatus*.[9] For in the strict practice of the Tantric tradition the male orgasm is altogether withheld for the use of a type of Yoga which the Westerner cannot easily manage without an experienced teacher. But if one is not intending to pursue the matter this far, it would seem best to let the orgasm happen in its own time, unforced by mental imagery or bodily motion. Beyond this, a couple following the strict tradition would perform *pranayama*—a special rhythm of breathing accompanied by the feeling that sexual energy is being sucked up through the spinal column toward the brain. By Hindus this energy is called *kundalini*, the serpent-power, and by Buddhists the *bodhicitta*, awakened awareness. It is supposed to be drawn up through the *sushumna* or spinal canal, passing on its way through various *chakra* or "wheels," representing plexi or centers of energy in the subtle body, which is how you *feel* to yourself as distinct from how you *see* yourself or are seen, in a mirror or through others' eyes or under a surgeon's scalpel. We must not therefore confuse

8. C. M. Chen, *Discriminations Between Buddhist and Hindu Tantras* (Mani Printing Works, Kalimpong 1969), pp. 207–208. Both the English and the typography of the original are such that I have had to take considerable liberties in transcribing this passage.

9. Incidentally, the female partner in *maithuna-yoga* is normally one's wife, though in exceptional circumstances, as when the wife has no concern for Yoga, the *shakti* or *dakini* is a particular woman selected by the *guru*. Supposedly, no issue comes of this union, and it is a general assumption of Indian folk-wisdom that chastity is always maintained so long as there is no actual emission of semen.

Konarak. Fourth south wheel.

Konarak. Figures from the hubs of the wheels.

the *chakra* system with the nervous system. The imagery of drawing energy up to the brain and, in its course, awakening latent centers of awareness is rather a symbolic map of a method of Yoga.

That a method with a goal is involved here suggests the nature of the life-problem which is being dissolved. It began as the "problem" of sexual lust, and now it continues as the problem of power lust. For as the *kundalini* follows its upward course it is said to arouse modes of consciousness in which there are sensations or manifestations of such psychic powers as telepathy, clairvoyance, telekinesis, and knowledge and control of the past and future. The temptation here is to aspire to full control of one's life, to dominate the course of events. Yet, it is easy to see that—for example—a completely known and controlled future is already past. You've had it. If you could really get what you want, wouldn't it have to include surprises? If so, because there are plenty of those already perhaps you are getting what you want already. But, thus, if you were to feel that everything is under your voluntary control, you would realize that you are voluntarily allowing things to happen in-voluntarily. Otherwise, you would not be able to know—by contrast —how it feels to act voluntarily. Similarly, you would not know that you are alive unless you had already known death, for how did it feel before you were born? It is, surely, that in nonverbal and nonconceptual awareness we see all the mutual interdependencies of processes which are distinguished and separated by words. When the urge of the male *is* the surrender of the female, the voluntary is the involuntary, and the movement of the figure is the movement of the background. When you fall, the ground jumps at you; when you rise, the ground drops.

This transcendence of opposites as an immediate experience beyond theory is, through the disciplines of Hinduism and Buddhism, the principal contribution of India to human wisdom.

Konarak. Over the rim of a wheel.

And then what? Is the outcome of such wisdom, as we generally suppose, only the immense urban and rural slum which is modern India? Would technologically competent and economically productive people ever have imagined that the need to survive, to expand through as much time as possible, is simply a concept and not a necessary feature of reality? If we judge by Western standards, we must first acknowledge that the Indian subcontinent has been actively populated, civilized, and exploited for three thousand years. It is thus eroded, deforested, and tired land, and its civilization can no longer afford such monuments as Konarak. But what took three thousand years to occur in India is being accomplished by us in one hundred and fifty, for, if we reckon the middle of the nineteenth century as the serious beginning of the industrial revolution, we shall in our present mode of progress have succeeded in reducing the North American continent to a desert by A.D. 2000. And this is without taking into consideration such contributions to human survival as the technologies of nuclear, chemical, and biological warfare.

India is not by any means a country of yogis, just as the United States is not a country of scientists. Must one keep on stressing the point that such generalizations as "Indian culture" and "Western science" describe only the activities of influential minorities, who, from time to time, succeed in catching the attention of practical players of the power and sex games? For the real winners in such games—the emperors like Ashoka and the bankers like Lorenzo de' Medici—are always troubled by the *hintergedanke* (a persistent thought far in the back of the mind) that their success is unreal. So long as this basic doubt remains unresolved their game-playing is frantic and ruthless, but if they can in some way realize that government, commerce, the stock market, and sexual dalliance are *only* games, they can continue to play with aristocratic detachment and generosity. This is the old Chinese ideal of being "king without and sage within." Similarly, in Sanskrit the word *chakravartin* (wheel-turner) may be applied both to an emperor and a buddha. This, too, is the whole point of the *Bhagavad-Gita*, for Krishna is showing the warrior prince Arjuna that even war—the most serious and dreadful of human pursuits—is only a game.

> You grieve for those for whom you should not grieve, and yet you talk of wisdom. The wise grieve neither for the living nor the dead.
> There was never a time when I was not, nor you, nor these princes, nor will there come a time when we shall cease.
> As this embodiment passes through childhood, youth, and age, even so is passage to another body. This does not trouble the sage. . . .
> Understand that That by which all this is pervaded cannot be destroyed. Destruction of the imperishable, none can achieve.
> It is said that these bodies of the eternally embodied [one] which is undestructible and unfathomable come to an end. Therefore fight, O Bharata!
> He who thinks that this one slays and he who deems that one as slain—both fail to see the truth: this one neither slays nor is slain.
> He is never born, nor does he ever die; nor, having existed, does he ever cease to exist. He is unborn, eternal, permanent, and primordial—not slain when the body is slain.[10]

This attitude toward the warrior's art is, perhaps, intelligible in societies where warfare is a regular and practical extension of politics, as, for example, when the Japanese *samurai* practice Zen Buddhism to improve their skill with the sword. But in an age when warfare is nothing but immense waste, and the deliberate slaughter of noncombatants, it is mutual suicide; there is neither ethical nor practical justification for it. Only a completely irresponsible madman could initiate nuclear war, but, from the standpoint of Yoga with its, shall we say, "nitty-gritty" approach to reality, this would be a natural catastrophe—as if the sun were to explode. And then, in the course of no matter how many aeons, cosmic energy would again reform itself into the patterns of intelligent

10. *Bhagavad-Gita*, II. 11–13, 17–20

life, playing again and again the theme, the sensation, which one calls "I myself here and now." One who realizes this fully takes no desperate measures to defend himself.

The philosophy of the *Gita* in respect to the destructive activity of warfare has, then, its parallel in the Tantric attitude to the creative activity of sexual union. It is simply the development of what was implicit in the philosophy of the Upanishads, and is even explicit in the *Chandogya Upanishad* (not later than 300 B.C.):

> Man issues forth from bodily identification to assume his real form upon attainment of the great illumination. Such a man is best among men. He lives like a king—eating, playing, and enjoying women or chariots or friends, without identification with the [idea of the] body. (8. 12. 3.)

This could well be the scriptural precedent for the whole construction of Konarak. For the temple is built in the form of an enormous chariot in which Surya, the Sun God is going on his diurnal "joy ride." On its twenty (originally twenty-four?) huge wheels a central, elaborately sculptured pyramid is supported by hundreds of caryatids—*apsaras* (celestial courtesans), *devas* (angel-gods), *nagas* (serpent equivalents of mermen and mermaids), *yakshas* (genii), and *gandharvas* (celestial musicians). Most of them are engaged in some form of sexual play—copulation, masturbation, cunnilinctus, fellatio, fondling, kissing, and enticing —the leptosomic *apsaras* with their full hemispherical bosoms, narrow waists, and curvaceous buttocks hanging like vines upon their lovers. Actually, the image is more of a float than a chariot—an ancient and no-holds-barred version of a Mardi Gras vehicle—for the entire scene is no other than the archetypal orgy or "holy-day," the sabbath which is "time-out" from the normal conventions and regulations of society.

There is a mirror-image relationship between the periodical orgy

(*Pages 102-103*)
Konarak.

(*Pages 104-105*)
 Serpent kings and erotic couples arrayed
on north wall of *shikhara*.

Konarak.

Konarak.

and the liberation from *maya* attained in Yoga, for both are situations in which proprieties, classifications, and conventions are transcended. Thus the former may be taken to represent the latter. In the orgy the whole familial and property-structured organization of society is temporarily abandoned in shameless copulation with strangers. In other words, the individual becomes an organism instead of a person with name, title, status, role, and property. Personality is cast off along with clothes, and the *Gita* points out the analogy in the famous verse:

> Just as one casts off worn-out clothes and puts on others which are new, even so does the embodied [one] cast off worn-out bodies and put on others that are new. (II. 22.)

To be shameless is to have no qualms about losing "face" or caste. It is thus the analogue of the selflessness, spiritual poverty, and (sometimes literal) nakedness of the yogi.

Should it, however, be said that the periodic orgy is a demonic parody of its spiritual analogue, that it represents a state as far below personality as *moksha*, or liberation, is above it? The problem is not as easily resolved as it might seem. Obviously, the occasional orgy can be afforded only by a very secure society, just as jokes about religion can be easily bandied by people of genuine and deep faith. But to what extent is the occasional orgy a necessary institution of the secure society? After all, even the holiest communities must make provision for eating, excreting, and sleeping—for what are called the "basic" and "animal" needs of man. Yet what is basic is not necessarily base, and what is animal is not necessarily inhuman; there are many respects in which animals are far less antisocial in their behavior than men. Furthermore, the orgy depicted at Konarak is not of animals or men, but of angels and gods. Surya's float shows the divine will being done "as it is in heaven," where "among the angels there is neither marrying nor giving in marriage," where, in other words, love is not legal possession.

Konarak. The male figure is apparently a monk or *arhan*.

We return, then, to the point that our confusions about sexual morality are semantic, reducing themselves to confusions between symbolism and reality. Symbolically, we are still living in a flat-earth world where heaven is "up" and hell is "down." Thus the head is a superior, loftier, and, therefore, "better" organ than the relatively inferior, baser, and, therefore, "worse" organs of sex, which are, alas, associated with the organs of excretion—as if we did not also spit and vomit from the mouth or having running noses. The same sort of absurd association between white, light, and goodness, on the one hand, and between black, dark, and evil, on the other, supports prejudice against dark-skinned people. Yet we are now coming to speak of wisdom as "profound" rather than "lofty," and of "deep" rather than "high" thinking. On a global world the airplane goes "out" rather than "up," and "in" rather than "down." The heavens become "far-out" rather than "way-up."

Change the imagery. Looking at the fully extended human being, the organs of sex are more central than the head, and we have love making the world go around itself, as in the flower. The head becomes the organ which directs the peripheral appendages—tongue, teeth, hands, and feet—in their service to that generative center of delight and life where the opposition of male and female is reconciled, where the solid fills the spacious and the spacious includes the solid, where the convex is one with the concave, where the hub of the wheel grasps the axle, and where active energy pours itself out into passive fecundity. Come to think of it, there is nothing more metaphysical and spiritual than the symbolism of sexuality.

Which, then, is the more blasphemous—to see sexual union as an image of the divine ground of the universe, or to see it as mere fucking, as in the expression "Fuck you!" Of course, as in Latin the word *sacer* means both sacred and accursed, holy names are the most powerful cusswords. A "bloody fool" is a "'S–bloody (i.e., Christ's blood) fool" and to give someone "the be-Jesus" is to beat him up. Conversely, someone who says "Dearest one, I want you to fuck me" is using the same kind of word magic as one who says either "Jesus, I love you!" or "Lord Jesus Christ, Son of God, have mercy!"

To the conventional Western Christian, the above paragraph may be even more offensive than the notion of drinking urine, but this is the very measure of our spiritual schizophrenia. We are dangerously insane and making ready to commit global suicide because we have separated the spiritual from the sexual, and the conceptual from the real. Obviously, only those who believe that the world of spirit is more real than the world of life, biology, and sex will gamble on detonating the atomic bomb. This applies equally to the prudish varieties of Hindus and Buddhists.[11]

In the light of this changed imagery, which makes the generative organs central instead of inferior, look again at Konarak. Seen from the air, the pyramidal center of Surya's float is a *mandala*, a fourfold flower-form image, which in plane may be considered female and in elevation male, the opening and the penetrating, the yielding and the firm. The *mandala*, or its more abstract form the *yantra*, is used throughout the Hindu-Buddhist world—and elsewhere—as a symbol of integration, centering, wholeness, and illumination, and in Yoga is commonly used as a focal image for contemplation. Thus in their lovemaking all the couples on the float are repeating the *mandala* theme, as the stars seem to repeat the sun, and everywhere the female hub rotates on the male axle.

Looking at these images, the beholder is invited, not to think, but to *feel* what all the couples are feeling, as described above by C. M. Chen. Paradoxical as it may seem, this nonconceptual and immediate feeling of the penetrating axle in the yielding hub may be represented in the more abstract image of the *sri yantra*.

11. Needless to say, it can be argued that the "population bomb" can destroy us just as effectively as the atomic bomb. But, quite aside from the promise offered by the techniques of contraception, what would be the possibilities of conditioning ourselves into the feeling that prolonged sexual arousal and contact, in the male, is even more delightful than orgasm? We are not as yet in a position to answer, but it must certainly be investigated.

For, as Ajit Mookerjee has shown,[12] this *yantra* must be understood as a finely tuned musical instrument whose strings represent all the energy-vibrations of the universe, and, according to Philip Rawson,[13] it does indeed correspond formally with the male *ragas* (mood scales) and female *raginis* of Indian music. In listening intently to this music I have always felt that the artists are plucking my nerves rather than strings, or that they are angels playing with the basic vibrations of the world. I feel that I am hearing immemorially ancient sounds from long, long ago which remind me, with what might be called a metaphysical nostalgia, of where I really came from and what all this universe is about. The feeling is the same as in *maithuna-yoga*—that she and I are lifted out of this particular time and place to somewhere "nowever," which at first emerges through the impression that all this has happened before, again and again, back and back to the very origin of time. But this origin is not actually "past," except in the sense that the musical instrument exists before or, rather, *underlies* anything played upon it.

It is thus that when Hindu philosophy states that everything is fundamentally *shabda*, or sound, it is talking about the basic pulse of energy which is differentiated, as light by the prism, through all our modes of perception. Upon this eternal harp, loom, or spectrum is played, woven, or seen—by the contrasts of sound and silence, warp and woof, light and darkness—the whole transient *maya* of our cosmos. But its desired delights and dreaded terrors are all of one sound, one cloth, and one vision.

12. *Tantra Art: Its Philosophy and Physics* (Kumar Gallery. New Delhi, New York & Paris, 1963), p. 21.
13. *Music and Dance in Indian Art* (Royal Scottish Museum. Edinburgh, 1963).

Khajuraho. Circa A.D. 100. Wall figures.

Khajuraho.

Khajuraho. Vishvanatha temple. The ideal of the supremely virile man giving delight to three women at once, and not merely pleasing himself.

Khajuraho. Frieze.

122   Khajuraho. Figures in front, *shardula*, modified
lion form representing power over nature, and
the release from bondage of nature.

Khajuraho. Vishnu as the cosmic boar. Decorations   123
on his body represent the cosmos.

Khajuraho. Maithuna A.D. 1000. Chitragupta
temple.